It is said by the Yoruba of Nigeria that the world began at Ile-Ife, the ancient city of the Yoruba peoples. There was only water and mist—no land or living creatures. One day, the almighty god Olodumare sent down one of the gods to the watery world below to create life. The god descended on an iron chain, carrying a gourd filled with earth, a hen, and a chameleon. When he arrived, the deity poured the earth from the gourd upon the water. Wherever the hen scratched at the earth, dry land formed. Then the chameleon walked upon the land to test its firmness. Soon other gods came to prepare the way for civilization.

The Yoruba peoples of Nigeria often describe the world as two connecting halves of a gourd—one half being the *orun* or spirit world, and the other half representing the *aye*, or earthly realm. As in the Yoruba myth above, these two worlds are linked together. All things in these two realms—gods, spirits, humans, animals, rivers, even words—possess something called *ase*, or life force. This powerful energy, which is expressed in Yoruba art and ritual, is the chain that connects the earthly world with the world of the spirits.

▲ Sango dance wand. The double-axis form at the top of this wooden dance wand symbolizes the power of Sango, god of thunder and lightning. Worshippers of Sango carry this wand as they dance.

Pronunciations

Yoruba is a "tonal" language. Capitalized letters indicate a higher pitch rather than an emphasis on the syllable.

Yoruba (yor roo bah)
Olodumare
  (oh LOH doo mahr ray)
Orun   (oh roon)
Aye   (ah yeh)
Ase   (ah sheh)
Sango   (shahn GOH)
Owo   (oh woh)
Oyo   (oh YOH)
Ogun   (oh GOON)
Ijebu   (ee jeh boo)
Oduduwa
  (oh doo DOO wah)
Hausa   (how sah)
Igbo   (ee boh)
Ijebu-Ode
  (ee jeh buh deh)

▲ These two Americans, a Yoruba priestess and priest, are participating in an annual Yoruba ceremony in Brooklyn, New York.

Nigeria, a "sub-Saharan" country in West Africa, derives its name from the river Niger, which crosses the country from the northwest to the south. There are many different ethnic groups living in Nigeria. In this book, we will look at the Yoruba, an ancient people whose remarkable culture has influenced and enriched other cultures throughout the world.

Ancient Kingdoms

As early as the twelfth century, the Yoruba lived in highly advanced city-states, ruled by sacred kings and queens. Ile-Ife, the oldest of all city-states, has maintained a dynasty of rulers that has remained unbroken to this day. Southeastern Owo was noted particularly for its dynamic cultural exchange with neighboring Benin. Oyo, situated near the Ogun River, was known for its fierce cavalry and trading power.

The Diaspora

The Ijebu kingdom, located along the southwestern coast, were the first Yoruba to establish trade with Europeans in the fifteenth century. At first, this commercial exchange increased prosperity for the Yoruba. But by the sixteenth century, the trade of goods had turned into a devastating trade of human lives. Millions of Yoruba (and countless other Africans) were forced into slavery and sent to work on large plantations across the Atlantic. Most Yoruba peoples were sent to the Americas—the United States, Haiti, Cuba, Trinidad, and Brazil. Many did not survive the voyage. The slave trade contributed to the discord among the Yoruba peoples, leading eventually to British colonial rule. This "diaspora," or dispersal of millions of African people, has had a profound affect on world culture. Today, elements of Yoruba art, ritual, music, dance, and religion can be seen flourishing throughout North and South America and the Caribbean.

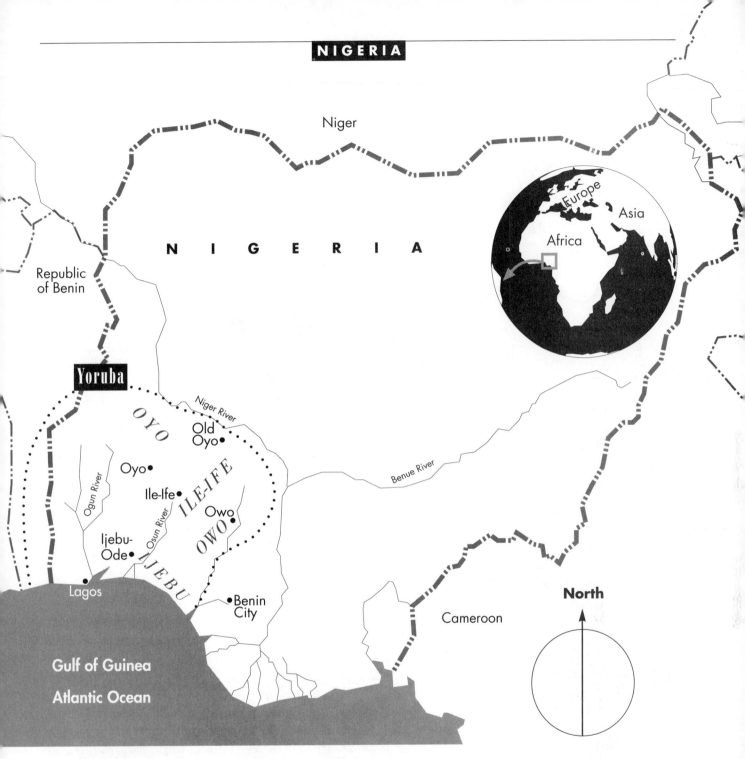

Niger

NIGERIA

Europe
Asia
Africa

Republic
of Benin

Yoruba

Niger River

OYO

Old
Oyo

Oyo

Ile-Ife

ILE-IFE

Ogun River

Osun River

Owo

OWO

Benue River

Ijebu-
Ode

IJEBU

Lagos

Benin
City

Cameroon

North

Gulf of Guinea

Atlantic Ocean

Besides the Yoruba, there are many other ethnic groups living in Nigeria. Two of the largest are the Hausa and the Igbo. The Hausa people live throughout the north and the Igbo occupy the southeast region beyond Benin City.

In ancient times, Ile-Ife, Ijebu-Ode, Owo, and Oyo were "city-states"—self-governing states consisting of a city and surrounding territory. Today, they are major Yoruba towns. A number of the rulers in these areas claim that they can trace their descendancy from Oduduwa, the first Yoruba king of Ile-Ife and founder of the Yoruba peoples.

3

▲ Weaving

In Nigeria, weaving is done by both men and women. Women weave with upright looms, like the one shown here, while men use horizontal ones. Home-spun cotton that has been dyed is most commonly used to create the often brightly colored and patterned Yoruba fabrics.

▲ Wood Carving

When creating a large sculpture, a master carver uses an adze to rough out a figure from one solid piece of wood. The detail work is done by apprentices. *Iroko*, a hard west African wood, is used for large carvings.

▲ Women's Clothing

The woman shown here is wearing *aso alaro* cloth, which is worn on special occasions. Her traditional outfit includes a wrapper around her waist, a blouse, another cloth which is held or placed over the shoulder, and a *gele*, or head-tie.

▲ Beadworking

Yoruba beadworking is a highly skilled craft done by men. The beadworker shown here is laying down threads of brightly colored beads over a conical structure to create a king's crown. Many important ritual objects involve beadwork, such as dance panels worn by priestesses, shrines, crowns, staffs, royal footstools, and clothing for sacred twin figures (see pages 6-7).

◀ Cooking

When preparing for a large feast, pounded boiled yams, a Yoruba staple, are formed into balls and wrapped in leaves to preserve their moisture. The yams are served with a delicious soup made with fish or chicken, okra, and melon seeds. In rural areas, cooking is done outside over large wood fires in back of the main house.

▲ Men's Clothing

On important occasions, men wear trousers made from strip-woven cloth, an embroidered *agbada*, and a hat.

5

▲ A *babalawo* practicing *Ifa*, a ritual which helps in assisting individuals or groups in times of need.

▲ Twins are sacred in Yoruba society. This woman is the caretaker of these two *ibeji* figures, which were created to honor her relatives' deceased twins.

There is an old Yoruba saying that the world is a market place we visit and the "Otherworld" is home. For those who follow a traditional belief system, their ritual life is a way to maintain a balance between the competing forces of both worlds. Performing rituals is also a way to pay tribute to one's ancestors and to ensure the continuation of Yoruba culture. To the Yoruba, art is not separate from ritual. Whether it is a dance costume, mask, or carving, every object is believed to possess "ase," the divine life force. This force is the energy that can bring about change in the individual and the community.

Divination

Divination, or *Ifa* (ee FAH), is a complex ritual used when one needs guidance or at times of personal or group crisis. The priests who perform Ifa are wise individuals who are able to use their ase for the benefit of others. The "diviner" or *babalawo* (bah bah LAH woh) uses a wooden divining tray carved with many images to assist in communicating with the spirit world. These carved figures refer to the entire cosmos—the Otherworld, mythic events, and everyday concerns. At the beginning of Ifa, the babalawo draws two intersecting lines on the surface of the tray, which has been sprinkled with dust. This is done to "open" the channels of communication with the spirit world. The point where these two lines meet symbolizes the crossroads between the two realms. After opening up communication, the babalawo then "casts" Ifa by grasping sixteen palm nuts from one hand to the other several times. One or two marks are made in the dust after each round. After two rows of marks are made, the total number dictates which sacred poem the babalawo should chant. By reflecting upon the poetry of Ifa, the individual seeking guidance can come to an understanding of his or her problem. Further divination then determines what sacrifices need to be made for addressing the problem through the help of the gods, ancestors, or other spirits.

Twins

In Nigeria, twins are regarded as "spirit children"—they are believed to possess special powers and can bring good luck. If a twin should die, the parents often have an *ibeji* (ee bay jee) figure carved to honor the dead twin. In order to ensure continued blessings from the twin's spirit, this memorial figure is ritualistically bathed, fed, and clothed for generations and generations.

Ancestor Worship

In Yoruba culture, ancestors are believed to be departed but not dead. The spirits of departed ancestors constantly influence the lives of the living by giving guidance and support when needed. Ancestor spirits are called on to help during divination rituals. People also pray to their ancestors and show respect by singing praise-songs when they worship at shrines. During the Egungun (eh GOON GOON) festival, the spirits of departed ancestors are honored in elaborate masked dances. (See page 16.) It is believed that during these dances, the ancestral spirits enter the dancers and their costumes. Like all Yoruba rituals, the objects used in the colorful and dramatic Egungun festival—from drums and dance staffs to brilliant fabrics—are considered to be dynamic expressions of ase.

▲ Egungun masquerader at the palace of a king in the Ijebu region. Each Egungun is associated with a different ancestral spirit. Most Egungun costumes are spectacular, made from hundreds of brightly colored cloth panels.

The Origin of Turtle's Shell

Long ago, Turtle had a beautiful smooth shell. He was admired far and wide for his beauty, but despised for his arrogance. His only true friend was Eagle, who was perhaps too dim-witted to notice Turtle's boasting. One day, Turtle said to Eagle, "I would be the happiest turtle on earth if only I could fly like you!" Turtle secretly felt inferior to Eagle because of his ability to fly. Eagle, feeling sorry for his friend told him, "Don't worry—I will figure out a way to help you fly, I promise!"

The next day, Eagle told Turtle to get on his back and hold on tightly. Eagle took off into the sky, flying higher and higher. Turtle was absolutely thrilled! He had never felt such joy and excitement before. From that point on, Eagle took Turtle up in the air every day. But soon Turtle's boastful nature got the best of him. He began to brag in the animal community about his "flying ability." Smart Hare became so jealous of Turtle that he refused to talk to him anymore. Powerful Elephant felt very small and inferior because he could not fly. His Majesty the Lion was upset and spent a lot of time wishing he were a turtle instead of a lion.

Turtle mercilessly taunted the birds in the community. He teased the ducks by saying, "Why, just yesterday I flew miles above you! You must be too fat to reach the clouds!" The ducks replied, "You're just a turtle! You can't possibly fly!" But when Turtle described what it was like up in the air, the ducks hung their heads in shame.

Soon everyone was talking about Turtle's remarkable talent. Word got back to Eagle, who naturally felt betrayed. On one of their flights, Eagle complained to Turtle, "Why do you spread these lies about how well you can fly? You know you have never flown by yourself!"

From *Ancient and Living Cultures Series: West Africa: Nigeria* published by GoodYearBooks. Copyright ©1994 Mira Bartók and Christine Ronan.

Proud Turtle was extremely insulted. "I can fly as high as you and that is that!" insisted Turtle. "What are you talking about?!" exclaimed Eagle. "Without me you are nothing in the air!"

"Are you challenging me to a test?" asked Turtle. "No!" cried Eagle. "You are my friend and I do not want you to risk your life to prove some silly point." But stubborn Turtle had actually convinced himself that he could fly. "I will prove it right now!" he shouted as he let go of his grip around Eagle's neck. Turtle hurled straight to the ground, causing his shell to break into bits and pieces.

Turtle lay on the ground for awhile groaning in pain and calling out for help. Nearby, a colony of black ants was building a new village. Hearing Turtle's cries, they rushed to his side. "We will do the best we can to repair your shell," said the head ant, "but we can't promise you that it will be perfect." "Fine, fine," said Turtle impatiently. "Just get started!"

So the ants went to work, gluing Turtle's shell together. Soon it was all in one piece and Turtle's body stopped aching. But Turtle still had not learned his lesson! Just as the ants were about to begin polishing Turtle's shell, Turtle exclaimed, "Don't you ants ever bathe? You smell terrible!" Angry and insulted, the ants packed up their tools and walked away. Turtle was left with a rough and ugly shell, which is the way it still looks today.

From *Ancient and Living Cultures Series: West Africa: Nigeria* published by GoodYearBooks. Copyright ©1994 Mira Bartók and Christine Ronan.

The Language of Proverbs

African proverbs are short statements filled with wisdom. Elegant and ageless, they come from careful observation of nature, animals, and everyday experiences. Proverbs are used in Yoruba speech to express many things—to settle a dispute, to teach social values and proper attitudes, or to stress the importance of belief. Proverbs are also related to the musical language of the "Talking Drum." (See page 22.) Read the following proverbs and see if you can understand the meaning behind them.

"The river is never at rest."

"The chameleon has given birth to its offspring—it is left to the offspring to learn how to dance."

"Two rams cannot drink from the same bowl."

"He who has hands but does not work is the father of thieves."

"One man has a head but has no cap—another man has a cap but has no head."

"As a person spreads his mat, so he will lie on it."

For centuries, the Yoruba of Nigeria have been making beautifully carved wooden sculptures, palace doors, and ritual objects. Many of these carvings, as well as fabrics, beaded objects, and ivory and metalwork, are elaborately

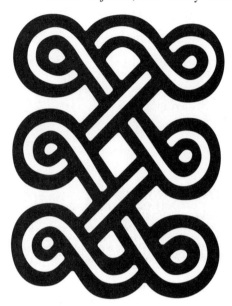

decorated with images of animals, birds, human beings, and geometric designs. Depending on the image, these designs symbolize many important concerns in Yoruba society— the power of their gods, or *orisa* (oh ree shah), the importance of leadership, fertility, the competing powers between this world and the spirit world, and the mystical power of women.

▲▼ Interlace Designs

There are many kinds of interlace designs in Yoruba art. The interlace is an ancient symbol that is usually found on objects associated with leaders—kings, rulers, priests, and priestesses. This symbol seems to be everywhere, painted onto gourds, embroidered onto ritual cloth, or carved onto

the door of a king's palace. The interlace is thought to be related to another common Yoruba symbol, the intertwined snakes. This snake design, which resembles the interlace in its twisting and turning of two forms, represents the play between the conflicting forces of everyday life.

▶ Fish-legged figure

This fantastic image of a
person with fish tails for
legs seems to appear
everywhere in Yoruba art.
Sometimes shown with a
bird or another creature
on its head, this figure is
viewed as a symbol of
authority and mystical
power. It is carved on the
lead *gbedu* (beh doo) drum
which is played for the
king. The fish-legged
figure that decorates this
kind of drum is often used
to symbolize Olokun (oh loh koon), goddess of the sea.

▶ Snake

Yoruba art is filled with images of snakes—entwined snakes
devouring each other, serpents grasping antelopes (symbols
of water spirits), and coiled snakes like the one shown here.
The coiled snake symbolizes
the python, regarded as the
great ancestor of all water
spirits. These water spirits are
said to live in rich and
fantastical palaces beneath the
sea. The snake is a versatile
creature with the ability to
operate in two separate
realms—on both land and
water. Because of this, the
snake is more powerful than
many other creatures.

 **The Origin of Twins**

A Yoruba Tale

There was a time in the
not so distant past when
human beings and animals
equally shared the wealth
of the world. No one took
more than their share, and
no one was superior to the
other. But one fatal day, a
farmer in Oyo began to
hunt monkeys. He would
hide in the bush while the
monkeys peacefully
gathered fruit, then sneak
up and attack them. Soon
the monkeys developed a
clever plan to get back at
the farmer. With their
special powers, they
caused the farmer's wife to
give birth to twins.
Unfortunately for the
farmer, the twins died. The
monkeys caused this to
happen many times. Each
time the farmer's wife gave
birth, she gave birth to
dead twins. Finally the
farmer decided to go to a
diviner for help. The
diviner scolded the farmer
for harassing the monkeys.
"The monkeys have sent
you *abiku*, children born to
die," said the diviner. "Let
the monkeys alone, or you
shall have sorrow all the
days of your lives." The
farmer saw the wisdom in
the diviner's words and
agreed to leave the
monkeys alone. And as
soon as he did, his wife
gave birth to a healthy
pair of beautiful twins.

Proving the Heron's Age

A Yoruba Tale

Long ago, there was a great dispute in the animal community. Both Chameleon and Heron claimed that they were the oldest of all the animals. In those days, to be old was the most respected thing of all. Time after time, public meetings were held to settle this dispute. Each time they ended in shouting matches between the two camps—the Pro-Chameleons and the Pro-Herons. The atmosphere in the community grew increasingly hostile. One day, some of the elders met secretly to discuss a way to end the disagreement once and for all. They told the antelope to go and notify Heron and Chameleon that they must appear before the public and present evidence of their ages. Both creatures accepted the challenge, and the community began to prepare for the big event. Before the public trial there was a great feast. Palm wine flowed freely, and the best cooks served dish after dish of delicacies. After some time, Lion signaled Elephant to silence the group. Elephant trumpeted loudly, and the trial began.

(continued on page 13)

◀ Ram

The image of the ram's head is a very ancient symbol in Yoruba art. It can be seen as far back as the eleventh century in the majestic terracotta and bronze sculptures of that period. Often used to represent a deceased ancestor, the ram is a symbol of power and leadership. The ram's ability to fight bravely and defend itself, combined with its qualities of strength and alertness, make it a powerful symbol. Among the Owo Yoruba, wooden sculptures of ram heads are often placed on ancestral altars. It is believed that the ase, or life force, of the ram's head can make communication with ancestral spirits possible.

▼ Equestrian figure

The equestrian figure, or horseback rider, is often associated with royalty and sacred political power. It is also a warrior symbol, referring to warfare and victory over one's enemies. During the expansion of the Oyo Yoruba empire in the seventeenth and eighteenth centuries, warriors held a particularly high status in society. This was largely due to the strength of the Oyo Yoruba cavalry. The equestrian figure has also traditionally been a symbol of prestige and wealth. In the past, those who were wealthy enough to own a horse were both respected and envied.

(continued from page 12)

▶ Chameleon

In Nigeria, "liminal" creatures, or animals that exist in more than one kind of environment, are highly respected. The chameleon is a small reptile that lives both in water and on land. The Yoruba believe that creatures like this have special powers because they possess abilities that humans do not. Some Yoruba associate liminal creatures with Esu (eh shu), an unpredictable god who, like the chameleon, moves in different realms. Because the chameleon camouflages itself in order to thwart its enemies, it is viewed as a symbol of transformation. Chameleons are also noted for their large eyes, which are seen as evidence that they are all-seeing and all-knowing.

▶ Bird

Also liminal creatures, birds have the ability to live in the air, on the ground, and sometimes, as in the case of the heron, on water. Certain birds are viewed by the Yoruba both as symbols of the diviner's ability to chant and the mystical power of women. The Yoruba word for mystically powerful women is *eleye* (eh leh YEH), or "owners of birds." Images of birds are used to decorate the king's beaded crown, representing female power and the king's need for women's support in order to rule. At the peak of the king's crown is the *Okin* (oh KEEN), or the "king of birds," whose long white tail feathers protrude majestically from the top. (See the photo on page 14.)

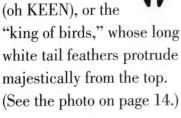

Chameleon was the first to go. He approached the platform, dancing back and forth in his strange little way. "I came into this world before any other animal," began Chameleon. "The Creator had just created land and it was too soft to walk on. That is how I developed this cautious way of walking. By the time the land got hard, I was used to this funny walk. I was here before all of you!" The Pro-Chameleons cheered as Chameleon walked back to his seat. Then Heron staggered forward, trying to keep his oversized head from falling to one side. "I applaud this *young* fellow on his presentation," began Heron, causing the Pro-Herons to laugh. "Well, I was here even before the dawn of creation! At that time, there was no land at all. When my mother died, there still was no land and I had to bury her inside my big head!" A murmur of amazement swept through the crowd. Then a unanimous cheer broke out and it was decided once and for all that Heron was the oldest of them all. But Chameleon never stopped wondering whether or not Heron's story was true.

◄ The king of Ila-Orangun, wearing the sacred beaded crown and holding a ritual staff, a symbol of authority.

The Yoruba say that the king of Ife, the ritual center of Yoruba culture, is a direct descendent of Oduduwa, one of the deities sent down to supervise the creation of the earth. According to legend, the arrival of Oduduwa marked the beginning of a long dynasty of rulers. In Yoruba society, the king, or *oba* (uh buh), represents the sacred link between the king's subjects and their gods and ancestors.

Since Nigeria's independence from Great Britain in 1960, the country has had a series of ruling political leaders, both military and civilian. Although the government exercises much power and authority in the various Nigerian states, the oba is the spiritual leader of the Yoruba. There are several oba in the Yoruba region of Nigeria, each ruling over a specific territory. The oba is aided by many people, including various chiefs and female palace officials. The female officials of the royal court play a central role in annual ceremonies. In some courts, these powerful elderly women, called *Iya Kere* (ee YAH kare reh), are the only ones allowed to place the sacred crown on the king's head. The crown symbolizes the very essence of sacred kingship and is treated with as much respect as the king. This elaborately beaded crown is adorned with many birds, which represent the support and cooperation of women.

Besides the crown and other royal objects, visual symbols of the oba's sacred authority can be seen throughout Yoruba culture, particularly in the form of the *ilekun* (ee leh koon), or palace door. These richly carved doors convey the king's importance with symbols of power and images from his everyday life.

▶ Early 20th century palace door, carved by the artist Areogun.

Make a Palace Door

Yoruba sculptors are considered to be some of the greatest woodcarvers in the world. By following simple directions, you can make and carve your own palace door, using Yoruba designs to decorate it.

Materials

- stencils
- 2 tablespoons of powdered alum (in your grocery's spice section)
- 2 tablespoons of vegetable oil
- 2 cups of flour
- 1 cup of salt
- 1 $^3/_4$ cup boiling water
- mixing bowl and spoon
- rolling pin
- rectangular piece of heavy cardboard, about 16" x 20"
- butter knife
- markers
- acrylic or tempera paints and brush

Directions

1. Mix the first five ingredients together in the bowl.

2. Roll the dough out onto the cardboard. The dough should be about $^1/_4$" thick. (**A**)

3. Place the stencils over the dough and partially carve out the empty spaces with the butter knife. (**B**) Experiment with textures by making different kinds of marks with the knife.

4. Wait about two days for the dough to dry completely. Then color your palace door with markers or paint. (**C**)

Discovery Questions

- Carving elaborate doors has been one way for Yoruba artists to make important public art. What kind of "public art" is displayed in your town or city?
- How is public art different than the art we see inside homes or museums?

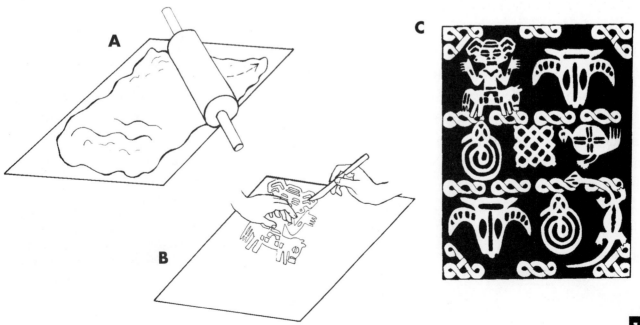

Egungun

In Yoruba, "Egungun" means "masquerade." Egungun are annual masquerade festivals that publically honor ancestral spirits. These rich and colorful festivals involve a series of elaborate masked dances and are celebrated throughout Yoruba culture during the dry season—December through March.

▲ Egungun dancers at a memorial ceremony for an important woman in the community.

The Egungun festival varies from town to town, depending on the ancestral history of the place. For example, if a town has a strong military history, the Egungun honored may be warrior spirits. The dancing and drumming might be very aggressive and chaotic, reflecting the war-like nature of the local ancestors. Costumes vary greatly as well, ranging from fantastic animal masks to spectacular costumes made of highly patterned cloth. Each Egungun costume covers the entire body of the masquerader because the ancestral spirit, who is believed to be concealed inside the cloth, is too sacred to be touched. Cloth is important in all Yoruba ritual. During Egungun, people "sacrifice" cloth to ancestors by placing it on shrines as a gift.

Gelede

In the rainy season, a festival called Gelede (geh leh DEH) takes place. Gelede honors the power of women, acknowledging their importance through masked dances. Gelede masks show an incredible variety. The groups of figures carved at the top of each mask can represent a historical event, make a moral statement, or even poke fun at a local incident. Like the Egungun festival, cloth plays a significant role during Gelede. Right before they perform, the male dancers borrow cloth from women and use it in their costumes.

▶ Unlike the Egungun dancers, Gelede dancers wear elaborately carved wooden headdresses.

Make a Mask

The figures on top of Gelede masks often make social comments about certain issues, people, or situations. By using the stencils and your own images, you can make a social statement on top of your head!

Materials

- stencils
- brown paper bag, large enough to fit over your head
- sturdy paper plate or disk of cardboard the size of a paper plate
- glue, tape, or stapler
- scissors
- sheet of thin posterboard
- colored markers
- twist-ties or pipe cleaners
- yarn, colored paper, beads, feathers (optional)

Directions

1. Trace the stencils on the posterboard. Cut out the stencil shapes and cut out some shapes of your own design. Leave tabs on the bottom of the shapes to attach to the plate. (**A**)

2. Attach the shapes to the plate or cardboard disk using staples, tape, or glue. Keep adding shapes, building the scene up. Cut slots in the shapes to attach other shapes. (**B**) Attach other materials if you want.

3. Put the bag over your head and carefully mark where you will need to cut eye holes.

4. Attach the sculpture to the top of the bag by carefully poking holes and inserting twist-ties or pipe cleaners. (**C**)

Discovery Question

- One way Yoruba society shows its openness is through the art of masquerade. Each region is free to practice religion in its own way, and this is reflected in the variety of masks and costumes. How does your culture show acceptance of different kinds of religious practices?

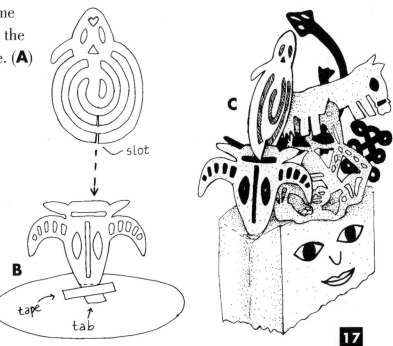

▲ This woman is wearing traditional *adire* cloth and a *gele*, or head-tie.

In Nigeria, the way one dresses is an outward expression of self-image and status. By the materials, patterns, style, and colors of one's clothing, a person can communicate his or her occupation, wealth, or membership in a particular social or religious group. "Traditional" dress tends to be layers of cloth wrapped and/or draped around the body. Men often wear a beautiful woven and embroidered gown called an *agbada* (ahg BAH DAH). To complement a woman's outfit, she often ties a *gele* (geh leh) on her head.

Adire (ah deer reh) cloth, which is a dyed indigo cotton fabric, is worn by women at the market or while doing domestic chores. Using a "resist" process, patterns are created by tin stencils or freehand drawing on the fabric. Cassava paste is used to resist the dark blue dye. Sometimes legends are illustrated on adire cloth, other times the patterns are commemorative images of leaders, political slogans, or simple geometric designs. Another kind of cloth, called *aso alaro* (ah sho ah lah ro), is worn on festive and important occasions. Aso alaro cloth is woven in strips on a loom.

Aside from clothing, cloth plays a significant role in ritual events and masquerades. During the annual Gelede festival, which honors the power of women, masqueraders collect strips of cloth to make up their costumes the day before they dance. Because of this, Gelede performers are often called "day borrowers of cloth." The possession of cloth is equated with wealth and is considered a "sacrifice" when given away. During the Egungun festival, thankful mothers offer their cloth as a sacred gift to ancestral spirits.

◀ Egungun masqueraders often use cloth to transform themselves from one spirit into another. While the Egungun whirls around, the cloth changes color and shape.

Make Adire Cloth

The Yoruba have different uses for their beautiful cloth—self-expression, commemoration, and ceremony. Pick the stencil designs you want to use to decorate your adire cloth and learn this fun dye-resist project.

Materials

- stencils
- piece of white cotton fabric 12" x 12"
- 2 paintbrushes: 1 fat, 1 thin
- vegetable shortening
- pencil
- dark blue acrylic paint
- small bowl for mixing paint
- water
- tape
- newspaper

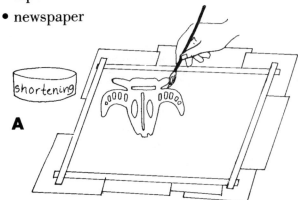

A

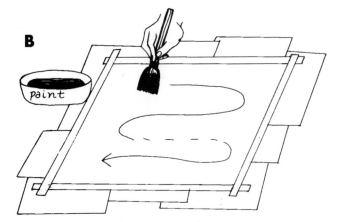

B

Directions

1. Tape the fabric to the newspaper, keeping it taut.

2. Using a pencil, lightly trace the stencils on the fabric.

3. Using the thin paintbrush, paint a thick layer of vegetable shortening on the design where you want the fabric to remain white. (**A**)

4. Thin the paint with a little water until it is the consistency of yogurt.

5. Using the wide paintbrush, paint the *entire* fabric. (**B**)

6. When the fabric is dry, peel it off the newspaper. Some newspaper may stick to the fabric, but this will be washed off in the next step.

7. Rinse your fabric in water with a little soap to remove the vegetable shortening and the newspaper bits.

Discovery Question

- Western culture has influenced African dress of today. How has African design influenced Western fashion?

C

Like clothing, body decoration can tell us a lot about a person—personality, economic class, or religious or social affiliation. Since ancient times, the Yoruba have placed great importance on personal appearance. Historical evidence shows that even before the first century, Yoruba peoples wore elaborate hairstyles, decorative pendants, and thick strands of beads and shells. They also have a strong tradition in highly decorative body tattooing, painting, and scarification—the scratching of designs onto the skin. Today, Yoruba style is a blend of clothing and jewelry design inherited from the ancient past, with influences from the Islamic, African, and Western world.

The material used to make jewelry has historically been an indication of a person's status. In the eighteenth-century Ijebu kingdom of southwestern Nigeria, royalty and high-ranking citizens wore well-crafted bronze bracelets and armlets with intricate designs as symbols of prestige. In the Owo kingdom, ivory, which comes from elephant tusks, was more widely used.

▲ This young woman's beads publically demonstrate her family's wealth and status. Her hair combs are also a mark of beauty.

▲ 17th century ivory armlet, showing the fish-legged figure. At one time, it was worn by a king.

Kings, chiefs, warriors, and diviners wore elaborately carved ivory bracelets like the one shown on the left. In Yoruba myth, Orunmila (oh ROON mee lah), the god of wisdom who is associated with diviners, is often described as using ivory objects. Olokun, another Yoruba deity, is associated with coral and is called the "giver of beads." Beads and cowrie shells have traditionally been signs of wealth and power, as well as an indication of personal well-being. In certain areas, young girls still display their wealth and family status at festivals by wearing countless strands of beads around their hips.

Make an Armlet

In the ancient kingdoms of Nigeria, only people of great power wore beautiful bronze or ivory armlets. Make and decorate your own piece of "royal" jewelry by using only paper and markers.

Materials

- stencils
- piece of paper, 8 $\frac{1}{2}$" x 11"
- heavy thread
- large sewing needle
- buttons, sequins, bells, and other decorative items to string on your armlet
- colored markers
- stapler, tape, or glue

Directions

1. On the piece of paper, make two lengthwise folds 2 $\frac{1}{2}$" from each edge, making a 3 $\frac{1}{2}$" x 11" strip. (**A**) Tape the folds down. (**B**)

2. Decorate the smooth side with stencils and markers.

3. Staple, tape, or glue ends together to fit your arm loosely. Make sure the armlet fits over your hand.

4. Using needle and thread, attach ornaments, allowing them to dangle from the armlet. (**C**)

Discovery Questions

- Every African culture has different traditions of body decoration. Find out more about this subject and compare other cultures with Nigeria.
- What do you do to "decorate" yourself?

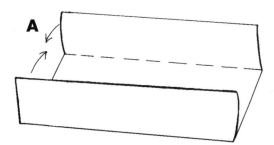

▶ A lead drummer playing a "talking drum," or *dundun* during an Egungun festival. The drummer is challenging the Egungun to dance well.

their complex rhythms. This is why the Yoruba are famous for their "talking drums," or *dundun* (DOON DOON). The dundun, which is played at most masquerades, is an hour-glass shaped drum with heads that are held together by leather thongs. These thongs, when pressed, change the drum's pitch, enabling the drummer to "talk" with his drum.

One cannot possibly separate drumming from the everyday life of the Yoruba peoples. Drums are played for all masquerades, commemorative events, weddings, funerals, and festivals. The drum is not simply an instrument used to keep a steady beat during a dance. It is used to play melodies and communicate proverbs, stories, and praises.

Much African music is actually derived from human speech. The Yoruba language is a "tonal" language, or a language based on the quality of sound. The "pitch" of the spoken word determines its meaning. For instance, the same word can mean different things, depending on how high or low portions of the word are pronounced. Yoruba drummers can actually duplicate human speech by changing the pitch in

The *bata* (bah TAH) is also played throughout Nigeria. Both ends of the bata are covered with goatskin, so it can be struck on either end. One end is larger than the other and is played with a leather stick while the other end is played with the hand. The bata is associated with Sango, a god who reveals himself through thunder and lightning. The bata drummer plays sharp notes, created to pierce the ear like lightning.

◀ This drum is sounded at the meetings of the Osugbo society, a group of elders that help solve problems in the community.

Make a Talking Drum

The Yoruba can communicate many things with their drums. With a few simple materials, you can make and decorate your own "talking" drum. Experiment with different sounds and try to communicate a message to a friend.

Materials

- stencils
- empty 5-gallon ice cream carton (most ice cream stores will give these to you for free)
- 1 yard of polyester lining material *OR* heavy brown paper
- 3 or 4 large rubber bands
- plain paper to wrap around the carton
- white glue
- water
- inexpensive paintbrush for applying glue (about 1" wide)
- scissors
- small bowl for mixing glue and water
- colored markers
- heavy twine or thin rope

Directions

1. Spread a little glue on the sides of the carton and cover it with plain paper. (**A**)

2. Stand the carton on the fabric or heavy paper and draw a circle around the carton and add a 4" border. (**B**)

3. Cut out the larger circle.

4. Put the rubber bands around the open end of the carton and roll them down a couple of inches.

5. Paint a glue strip around the open edge of the carton about 1" wide. Be sure to paint the lip of the carton too. (**B**)

6. Place the fabric or paper over the opening and pat the border into the glue. Pull the fabric or paper tight. Roll the rubber bands up and over the border. (**C**)

7. Mix glue and water to the consistency of milk (about two parts glue to one part water). Using broad even strokes, paint the glue mixture on the drum head. You can do this several times, allowing the glue to dry between each coat. Each time you do this, the sound of your drum will change. (**D**)

8. Decorate the drum with stencils and markers.

9. Tie two pieces of twine or rope around each end of your drum. Tie another piece between them to go around your neck.

10. Use sticks or pencils for strikers.

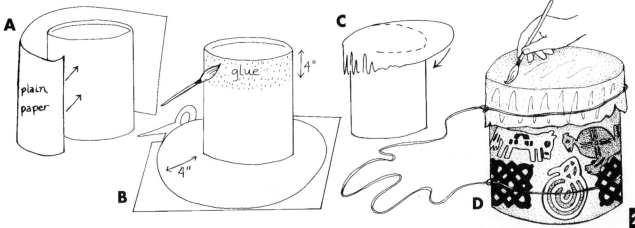

23

Books for Children

Areje, Raphael Adekunle. *Yoruba Proverbs.* Ibadan, Nigeria: Daystar Press, 1985.

Courlander, Harold. *Tales of Yoruba Gods and Heroes.* New York: Crown Publishers, 1973.

Ekwensi, Cyprian. *Drummer Boy.* New York: Cambridge University Press, 1967.

Kennerly, Karen. *The Slave Who Bought His Freedom, Equiano's Story.* New York: Dutton, 1971.

Price, Christine. *The Talking Drums of Africa.* New York: Scribner and Sons, 1975.

Schmidt, Nancy J. *Children's Fiction About Africa in English.* (Reference). Buffalo: Conch Publishing, 1980.

Books for Adults

Abrahams, Roger D. *African Folktales.* New York: Pantheon Books, 1983.

Drewal, Henry John, John Pemberton III, and Roland Abiodun. *Yoruba—Nine Centuries of African Art and Thought.* New York: Henry N. Abrams, Inc., 1989.

Drewal, Margaret Thompson. *Yoruba Ritual—Performers, Play, Agency.* Bloomington: Indiana University Press, 1992.

Thompson, Robert Farris. *Black Gods and Kings.* Bloomington: Indiana University Press, 1976.

Audio-Visual

A Day with Three Nigerian Second Graders. Slides. Center for African Studies, University of Illinois, 1208 West California, #101, Urbana, IL 61801.

Drums of the Yoruba of Nigeria. Music. Smithsonian Folkways Recording No. 4441. Smithsonian Institution, 955 L'Enfant Plaza, Suite 2600, Washington, DC 20560.

Folk Tales from West Africa. Cassette. Smithsonian Folkways Recording No. 7103. Address above.

Music of Africa. Film. Center for African Studies, University of Illinois. Address above.

Nigeria—A Short Introduction. Slides. Center for African Studies, University of Illinois. Address above.

Museums

The Art Institute of Chicago, Chicago, IL

The British Museum, London, England

The Detroit Institute of Art, Detroit, MI

The Ife Museum, Ile-Ife, Nigeria

The Metropolitan Museum of Art, New York, NY

The Museum for African Art, New York, NY

The National Museum, Lagos, Nigeria

National Museum of African Art, Smithsonian Institution, Washington, DC

New Orleans Museum of Art, New Orleans, LA

Seattle Art Museum, Seattle, WA

This book is dedicated to the Yoruba peoples of Nigeria, whose culture inspired its creation.

It is also dedicated to the teachers and children whose ideas and questions about other cultures were a catalyst for this series.

Other stencil books available in this Ancient and Living Cultures series are:
Ancient Celts,
Ancient Japan,
Ancient Mexico,
Indians of the Great Plains,
Northwest Coast Indians,
*Pueblo Indians of the
    Southwest,*
and
West Africa: Ghana.

Text is printed on recycled paper.

Portions of the royalties from the sale of this book will go towards developing educational programs in some of the cultures represented in this series.

$9.95

ANCIENT AND LIVING CULTURES

STENCILS

West Africa: Nigeria

This captivating activity book introduces children to the amazing and mythic world of the Yoruba peoples of Nigeria. Children will learn about Yoruba rites and rituals, masquerade, art, and music through five fun-filled art activities—a **mask, palace door, adire cloth, armlet,** and **talking drum.**

Also available in the Ancient and Living Cultures Series from GoodYearBooks are **Ancient Celts, Ancient Japan, Ancient Mexico, Indians of the Great Plains, Northwest Coast Indians, Pueblo Indians of the Southwest,** and **West Africa: Ghana.**

GoodYearBooks

*An Imprint of ScottForesman
A Division of HarperCollinsPublishers*

ISBN 0-673-36137-3